THE BEST OF

MATT

2003

D0505248

"I'd love to come for a pint, I'll just check with the 'pocket of resistance'"

MATTHEW PRITCHETT studied at St Martin's School of Art in London and first saw himself published in the *New Statesman* during one of its rare lapses from high seriousness. He has been the *Daily Telegraph*'s front-page pocket cartoonist since 1988. In 1995, 1996 and 1999 he was the winner of the Cartoon Arts Trust Award and in 1991 he was 'What the Papers Say' Cartoonist of the Year. In 1996, 1998 and 2000 he was *UK Press Gazette* Cartoonist of the Year and in 2002 he received an MBE.

The Daily Telegraph

THE BEST OF

2003

'Does my arsenal look
big in this?'

ORION

Orion Books
A division of the Orion Publishing Group Ltd
Orion House
5 Upper St Martin's Lane
London WC2H 9EA

First published by Orion Books in 2003

A CIP catalogue record for this book
is available from the British Library

ISBN 0 75285 788 6

Printed and bound in Great Britain by
Butler and Tanner, Frome and London

THE BEST OF

'*My name is Rex
and I chase foxes*'

War on Terror

'Bad news, sir, we think Saddam is stockpiling sand'

'I'd shoot myself in the foot if my gun wasn't jammed'

War on Terror

'I wish you wouldn't refer
to my mother as The
Grave and Gathering Danger'

War on Terror

'When did you decide to tighten up our security?'

War on Terror

'Taking on the Miss World responsibilities is overstretching the Army'

War on Terror

'Al Qa'eda has developed snow!'

'Is this a lamp or a chemical warhead?'

War on Terror

'It's Hans Blix – he says your glasses are in your coat pocket'

Terror threat

War on Terror

'The build up of TV military experts means that this war is almost unstoppable'

'... And stop smiling for the spy satellite photos'

War on Terror

Dodgy dossier

War on Terror

'*Asking my husband's opinion should always be seen as a last resort*'

War on Terror

'Any lunatic with a
microphone could set off
Clare Short again'

'We went to Calais for the
day to boycott French goods'

War on Terror

'Is it possible to be against the war and against the French?'

'Thank goodness for Clare Short – we need something to laugh about at the moment'

Will she, won't she, resign

War on Terror

'There's a school trip today –
I need an anti-war placard,
a whistle and a loud hailer'

Diplomatic crisis

War on Terror

'I've got a body double at home mowing the lawn'

'While the war is on we've hired our own military expert'

Search for Saddam

War on Terror

'It's full of sand'

War on Terror

'They've bombed Robin Cook's presidential palace'

Shock and Awe

War on Terror

'This continuous tapestry coverage makes it look like the battle is going badly'

'I still haven't decided on a role for him after the war'

24-hour news

War on Terror

'Oh no, it looks like Laurence Llewelyn Bowen has been here'

'Is that a real Saddam statue, or just a lookalike statue?'

War on Terror

'I looted it'

War on Terror

'It's hardly a weapon
of mass destruction'

'We must have an old leaving
card for Ms Short somewhere'

Finally, she goes

The Countryside

'You're coming on the Liberty March whether you like it or not'

The Countryside

'We believe the Countryside Alliance is only days away from developing placards'

Money

'No pension, no mortgage, no shares – suddenly I'm a financial genius'

'... About your nest egg – I've made you an omelette'

Money

'I've taken your savings out of the stock market. They're running in the 3.15 at Cheltenham'

'No occupational pension? I don't call that very wise'

Sporting Life

'But I've just
had my hair braided'

'For a while, Mr Beckham,
you'll only be able to
count up to five'

Law and Order

'I went out to congratulate a policeman but I couldn't find one'

'Oooh, does anyone else have déjà vu?'

Law and Order

'He paid for dinner but we went halves on the spot fine for rowdy behaviour'

Law and Order

'I'm looking for some music that glorifies harsher prison sentences'

'I'm not paying the fine and I'm armed'

Gun culture

Law and Order

'He just melted –
nobody shot him'

Fire Strike

'I'm in an awkward position – I work part-time at the Treasury'

The Royals

'A new tea towel? You've only
had that one for 50 years'

'I think we can rule out
housemaid's knee,
Your Majesty'

Golden Jubilee

The Royals

'Who sold you that?'

'How much for the hat?'

Gifts for sale

The Royals

'I told the Queen
I was parking here'

THESE
PREMISES ARE
GUARDED BY
PRINCESS
ANNE &
HER DOGS

Butler trial collapses . . . but Princess Anne is fined

The Health Service

'The hospital isn't much good, but I'm on one of the country's elite waiting lists'

'Sorry, sir, you can't come into a foundation hospital looking like that'

Student Fees

'I didn't get round to finishing it'

'Isn't that better than a university degree?'

Student Fees

'I will be from a poorer
family by the time
I graduate'

'How much for just
the scarf?'

Just Politics

'ROB THE RICH?
Have you cleared this
with Tony Blair?'

'So, Sir Denis, were you
surprised to discover that
God is a woman?'

Denis Thatcher dies

Just Politics

'I know we're the nasty party, but are we nasty in a traditional or modern way?'

Just Politics

'I'm writing a diary.
You're not in it'

'If Edwina had kept quiet
about salmonella I could
have become Tory leader'

Edwina's diary revelations

Just Politics

'We don't consider two Tories to be a calm and stable environment for a child'

'One day everyone will be leader of the Tory party for 15 minutes'

Just Politics

'SHOO!'

Just Politics

IDS – the quiet man
of politics . . .

'He's ditching his quiet
image and going for a
more humorous one'

. . . or not

Just Politics

'Cutting off my arm is the
only way to get out of this
Tory bonding weekend'

'I went into politics to
make a difference –
and now I have'

Just Politics

'Since we now have our evenings free, I thought I might try a spot of burglary'

Just Politics

'Do you have to bring
your lifestyle guru?'

'Oh no! I've landed on
one of Cherie Blair's
properties again'

Cherie's friends cause embarrassment

Just Politics

'Do you think it's possible to
have TOO much fun?'

'I like Mr Blair but his
holier-than-thou attitude
is hard to take'

Just Politics

'I've reshuffled our
responsibilities'

'We forecast that he'd
be 55 this year'

Just Politics

'Look, it's Tony Blair
concentrating on
domestic issues'

'Why do you have to drag
politics into everything?'

Prescott goes from Two Jags
to Two Fingers

Europe

'Why do you always have to personalise our differences about the euro?'

'They're not of crucial importance – just a tidying up matter'

EU Constitution

Europe

'I'm afraid you failed the test – but you made a lot of positive noises'

'My policy is yes but not yet'

Gordon Brown's Five Euro Tests

Foreign Affairs

'It's so irritating not being able to take one's owners abroad'

Foreign Affairs

Terror threat

Foreign Affairs

'Darling, I did it to help you
with your memoirs'

'I told you we should
have gone to Venice'

Hillary Clinton publishes
autobiography

Asylum

'I don't want 200,000 low-cost homes built in my backyard'

Asylum

'I suddenly feel terribly
depressed about the cricket'

'So, now we're not good
enough for them'

English Weather

'. . . the pollen count is high and there's a 90% chance of fat men with their shirts off'

'I came up the high street too quickly and now I've got the bends'

English Weather

Christmas floods

English Weather

'Can I keep him?'

'I've cloned a snowman'

The Church

'I'm a lapsed homosexual'

'Look, there's your boyfriend – as the actress said to the bishop'

Gay bishop row

And finally . . .

"We're remaking 'Brief Encounter' — there are no trains and it ends with a gay wedding"

And finally . . .

'There were three in favour and one against. The other 45,746 were illegible'

'Now you mention it, I think I might have a wife and family'

And finally . . .

'I think the University
of Life has been
marking me down'

And finally . . .

'Sorry I'm late,
I visited 2002 and
got caught in traffic'

'They must be
held up somewhere'

And finally . . .

And finally . . .

'...or for just £125,000 you can have this lovely photograph of a house'

And finally . . .

'If it's all right with the
shareholders I'd like
another cup of coffee'

Fat cats

And finally . . .

'Are we nearly there yet?...
Are we nearly there?'

'Go to bed or the Harry Potter
book gets it'

And finally . . .

'I've invented the
motor show'

'I suppose this is
goodbye, then'

And finally . . .

'Don't worry, if this goes wrong
I'll just call it a public autopsy'

'It makes a change from
buying him socks'

Bodyworks show

And finally . . .

'You were told to wear
sensible walking shoes
and bring a packed lunch'

'It's still shaking 24 hours
after the earthquake'

And finally . . .

'I'm trying to look worried,
but who am I kidding?'

'Oh bother'

And finally . . .

'I got a tickly cough and my
husband won a sponge cake'

Cheating quiz show Major

'Attendance has shot up
since the vicar got
a stun gun'

Muslim Cleric's
premises raided

And finally . . .

'Prisoners go out more
often than we do'

'I'm still looking
for a publisher'

And finally . . .

'Now can we have
Catherine Zeta Jones
with the judge's mother?'

'I wish you wouldn't grunt
when you use the
remote control'

Wedding photos . . .

And finally . . .

'After the kidney transplant
it insisted on a nose job'

Transplants for pets